"The One Prescription Y[...]

Prescripti[...]
Wealth

Why You Should (and can) Be Rich

By Dr. Tomas McFie

Published by Life Benefit$, Inc.
7871 Darling St SE Salem, OR 97317, U.S.A
1-866-502-2777 | 503-363-LIFE(5433) | team@life-benefits.com | www.life-benefits.com

First published, February 2011
First printed, February 2011

Printed in the United States of America
Edition: Second
Printing: First

ISBN: 978-0-9834757-6-7

Discounts are available for quantity purchases. Contact the publisher for details.

DISCLAIMER: Although the author and publisher have made every effort to ensure that the information in this book was correct at press time, the author and publisher do not assume and hereby disclaim any liability to any party for any loss, damage, or disruption caused by errors or omissions, whether such errors or omissions result from negligence, accident, or any other cause.

The views and opinions expressed in this book are for the sole purpose of guiding people to make educated decisions about their financial affairs and are not written by a certified financial planner. The author of this book has done diligent research in the field of financing but does not carry any authority, credentials or certifications to give financial advice. Nothing in this book constitutes or is meant to constitute advice of any kind. If you require advice in relation to any legal, financial or medical matters you should consult an appropriate professional.

Loans and withdrawals from life insurance can cause adverse tax consequences, penalties and may cause your policy to lapse. Insurance products are backed by the claims paying ability of the issuing insurance company and are not FDIC insured. Life Benefits, Inc., its agents, and representatives are not authorized to give legal or tax advice.

Table of Contents

Foreword...*i*

A Word of Acknowledgment.............................. *iii*

Dedication .... *v*

Introduction to the Second Edition ....*vii*

A Brief Introduction .... *ix*

Exposing the Mystique Surrounding Money..........*1*

Banking: An Essential of a Thriving Economy......*5*

The Solution *15*

The Process *19*

The Reason Why..*33*

Value of Protection *39*

Real Life vs. Theory...*43*

What Are Others Doing?.....................................*51*

"You Are Here" *59*

Stories from Clients..*63*

Glossary *75*

Index..*79*

References *81*

Foreword

Recently I was introduced to a nutritional product that said, "This product is a precursor" to taking a supplement that I had been taking earlier. In other words, I would get better results by taking this item first, and taking the other one later in the day.

Dr. Tom McFie (and his wonderful family) has written the perfect "precursor" to my book, <u>Becoming Your Own Banker – The Infinite Banking Concept.</u> Before reading my book, one should first read <u>Prescription For Wealth</u> by Dr. Tomas P. McFie! In fact, Tom says in the introduction, "Its main intent is to influence you to read <u>Becoming Your Own Banker.</u>

During the past ten years I have met thousands of people whose lives have been changed significantly for the better by practicing the principles that are in my book. No one is better at it than the McFie family. They are awesome!

His book is inspiring, witty and fun to read. It accomplishes his object beyond all expectations. All of his family "chipped in" to write this book. The back cover is a real delight. Since this is a <u>Prescription For Wealth</u> there is the usual "warning of side-effects." I particularly like the warning, "Keep this prescription in reach of your children at all times!"

R. Nelson Nash
-Author of <u>Becoming Your Own Banker</u>

A Word of Acknowledgment

"What has happened before will happen again. What has been done before will be done again. There is nothing new in the whole world."[1]

The first page and the last page of any document are often the first, and sometimes the only thing, to be read. Therefore I would encourage you to read this page and the last page right now. They contain the necessary information for you to learn what the title of this book is all about.

In fact in light of the above quotation, nothing in this book is new or unique. Most if not all of the content is what I have been taught by others.

You may be asking, "If everything has already been discussed and written before, why write it again?"
Well, hopefully the way I have expressed it here will help you on your path to real and lasting riches. You see, in the process of coaching hundreds of others in how to think and behave like an honest banker, I have found the information contained in this little book to be essential. So much so that without grasping this information people will often never implement the banking process in their lives.

So, thanks to everyone who has contributed to this project, indirectly or directly, your input has made the world a better place.

Now, beside this general thanks, I specifically want to thank: Drs. Tedd Koren and Terry Rondberg... your

---

[1] Ecclesiastes 1:9

diligent proofing and encouragement were priceless! With your prominent history of writing and publishing, it was an honor to have your help with this small work; My children who always work endlessly by my side not just throughout this writing, but also in designing the cover, proof reading and helping me to create Word documents on the computer. My friend and mentor Ray Poteet... for the path you have blazed for me and many others. Thank you!

Dedication

"A truly good wife is the most precious treasure a man can find!

"Her husband depends on her, and she never lets him down.

"She is good to him every day of her life...!.

"She is like a sailing ship that brings food from across the sea.

"She gets up to prepare food for her family and for her servants.

"She knows how to buy land and how to plant a vineyard, and she always works hard.

"She knows when to buy or sell, and she stays busy until late at night.

"She helps the poor and the needy.

"Her family has warm clothing, and so she doesn't worry when it snows.

"Everything she wears is beautiful.

"Her husband is well-known and respected.

"She makes clothes to sell to the shop owners. "She is strong and graceful, as well as cheerful about the future.

"Her words are sensible, and her advice is thoughtful.

"She takes good care of her family and is never lazy.

"Her children praise her, and with great pride her husband says, "'There are many good women, but you exceedingly are the best!'" [2]

Thank you Michele, you are the best!

---

[2] Proverbs 31:11-29

Introduction to the Second Edition

The response this book has received is truly humbling. Few weeks have passed, since it was first off the press, where multiple orders are not taken and processed for people all over the United States and around the globe.

This second edition is nearly identical to the first except for some minor correction to format issues and spelling errors. That is because the message is as true and powerful as it was when it was written.

The massive amount of feedback received from those who have read <u>Prescription for Wealth</u> has provided inspiration resulting in an additional work entitled <u>How to Win Your Financial G.A.M.E.</u>™ (YFG.)

<u>How to Win Your Financial G.A.M.E.</u>™ is a play by play guidebook for those who want to progress to their highest level of performance.

A Brief Introduction

There's nothing like a good 'ole robbery to shake your life up. At least that's the way it was for us in November of 2005. I received a phone call informing me not to come directly home that evening---our home had been robbed! The swat team and K-9 unit were still rummaging through and about our house trying to figure out, "who'd done it."

Up until then, my wife, the children and I, had been cruising along in life not living high on the hog, but still not suffering anything terrible. But we did have concerns about how to make things a little better and a little easier financially just the same. Having experienced some very discouraging results from conventional financial counsel over the years we were opportune candidates to pay attention to something unique.

You see my training was in chiropractic. I had been in practice for over 20 years at the time. We had owned 4 different clinics and had paid cash for nearly everything we owned up until that time, including our home. So we weren't in debt. Fact is, we'd taken a full year off in 1997, then in 2002 we traveled leisurely for three months across the southern part of the country to settle near our "home" state and started a brand new practice without incurring any debt.

And so when that call to the office came that November of 2005, informing me not to come home that evening, we were back living in Salem, Oregon.

But notwithstanding our travels, business success and life experiences, there seemed to be a missing link, some distant fear of the future, that hauntingly kept hanging around. As life moved along we seemed to progressively have to work harder and harder in order to maintain our commitment to remain debt free---simply because life happens! And then there were the major expenses on the horizon which seemed pretty overbearing and at times overwhelming ...college tuition for the children, weddings, our own retirement, etc.

No, we weren't naïve. We had consulted, pursued and implemented conventional financial planning advice aggressively. We had been actively involved in futures and option trading, real estate and had contributed to our IRA's, 401ks (actually a SEP as I was self-employed,) but there was no way those plans and investments were going to finance our lifestyle when we reached our golden years--- even our financial planner admitted to that with a sheepish shrug of his shoulders.

I'd been watching what happened to patients of mine who'd been "set for life" and looking forward to the freedom which had been promised them through conventional financial planning methods. Candidly I was distressed! Here were these wonderful people who had worked and saved their entire working lives and they were not able to even enjoy the same lifestyle they'd enjoyed while working. Why? Because the workers of deception (financial planners, dishonest bankers, politicians and social engineers) had stolen their golden years away from them with silly promises like; social security, 401ks, IRAs securities and the like. Pathetically, these false promises of hope had cost many of these wonderful people their very life because they couldn't afford the necessities regarding their own health when the plans didn't turn out the way they were told they would. Others become subject to shrewd business people who took advantage of them because they could no longer afford to keep their homes up to code, and city or state ordinances forced them to sell their homes for pennies on the dollar. Others lived their golden years from their cars as they couldn't afford the rent or mortgage payment any longer.

Along with this was the poor nutrition with which they suffered. Having become so financially strapped they could no longer afford their water and sewer bill let alone quality food products. In short many beautiful people right here in America, have had their golden years devastated because of the system which has caused them to trust others with their financial future instead of taking control of their own finances themselves. This is not something you want to duplicate.

You really can choose to continue to live by going places, doing things, seeing people and helping others fulfill their goals. You can choose to wear out instead of caving in. Retirement should not be your objective in life. And only you have the power to choose to never be in a position which would entice you to beg, borrow or steal from others[3] in order to live.

Now when that robbery occurred back in November of 2005, it opened a new chapter in my life, a break away from the same ol', same ol' because it forced me to look at things from an entirely different perspective. Let me share with you how it all happened.

In 2002 I had received a letter from a colleague of mine in Rome, Georgia. Dr. Bob Manna. Dr. Bob mentioned his friend from Kansas. Dr. Bob was writing about thankfulness and gratefulness and how those traits will build relationships, friendships and business. He mentioned his friend from Kansas because he said, "I don't know of anybody that expresses his thankfulness more than

---

[3] Proverbs 30: 8-9

my friend Ray. I never call, email or write to Ray without him expressing how thankful he is for our relationship. And besides that, Ray saved me $30,000 in taxes last year."

Now in 2002 I was too pre-occupied keeping up with the debt-free life we were living to give this letter a second thought. Fortunately however, I didn't toss the letter but had left it in a file in my desk drawer. As we were cleaning up from the robbery my wife, Michele, happened upon this letter and gently suggested that I contact Dr. Bob.

We were packing up for a vacation in San Diego when I placed that call to Dr. Bob. He emailed his friend and his friend emailed me. Through it all I purchased the book, Becoming Your Own Banker by R. Nelson Nash and had it shipped overnight so we could take it on our trip. Interestingly, the promptness and eagerness to serve illustrated the thankfulness and gratefulness that Dr. Bob had written about to me years ago in his letter.

The next day, as Michele packed for the trip, I sat--- or followed her around--- reading to her from this new book. I still remember the looks she kept giving me like--- would you please put that book down and help? I felt a bit guilty but realized that this book contained something powerful!

I had been a clandestine student of Austrian Economics since a high school instructor, Mr. Shimp, had introduced me to Ayn Rand, George Orwell, Aldous Huxley, amongst many others in the mid 1970's. Mr. Shimp was the son of immigrants who'd escaped the Bolsheviks' takeover of the Tsarist autocracy in Russia during 1917. My personal studies had led me to read the works of Leonard Read, Ludwig von Mises, Murray Rothbard, Lew Rockwell and Ron Paul. Furthermore, we were home educating our children even though (actually in spite of the fact that) my wife was a certified public school teacher because we wanted our children to think rather than to be taught what to think.

So really, needless to say at this point, I was impressed with Austrian Economists' ability to diagnose world epidemics --- economically, socially and politically---- but I was equally disappointed, and sometimes even distraught, to see that they didn't have a real solution--- a plausible treatment or prescription--- for the condition which they could so accurately diagnose.

But the book which I now held in my hands was entirely different from anything else I had ever read or heard. Here was the prescription, the "how to" guide on what could be done to correct the mess that we were in---politically, socially and economically. This book was nothing less than a personal guide to what my family and I could do which would nullify much of what we feared about the future. Finally, here was the prescription that could cure the disease which the Austrians had so accurately diagnosed.

Well, I finished reading the book on the beach in San Diego and then called my older children (ages 9-14) off the beach to come and listen to me read the book to them. They caught my enthusiasm even though I'm sure they didn't catch the entire message at that time. But that wasn't their fault. You see, I had failed to pass on to them what I had learned in my study of Austrian Economics. Really, when you know you've got a disease but have no treatment for the disease, it can be a little depressing. I figured, why trouble them with the diagnosis if there wasn't any cure. Beside, most folks were preaching that the Lord would return and save us all from the devastation that was coming anyway. So why worry about it...right? Wrong! That day on the beach was a wakeup call for me. I couldn't wait to get back home and get the treatment phase started.

Michele and I first thought that it would take 4 to 7 years to fully implement the treatment program that this new book was prescribing. And we were very excited knowing that 4 to 7 years can fly by fast. Our oldest was just 14 at the time and it only seemed like yesterday that he was born. So we reasoned that another 7 years wasn't that long off. But our main concern was this, where in the world were we to find the product that this treatment plan required? Where were we going to be able to find the tools that we needed?

We struck out on the internet in search of an answer to our impasse and were overwhelmed! Little did we realize that the solution to our dilemma was a simple product that was easily attainable. So after a lot of time and energy spent chasing around and researching different companies and products we placed a follow up call to Ray's office and learned that he'd already done the research for us and had the best product and the best companies that provided the tools we would need.

Well, we immediately purchased our first participating whole life insurance policy through Ray and shortly financed the payoff of the self-employment taxes which we owed for 2005. That first single finance project made us over $2,000.00 plus we got back all the money ($12,000) we had spent on the taxes as well...a total of over $14,000.00 in only 36 months. But the neat thing about it all was that I didn't have to work any harder or any longer than I was already working and neither did Michele! Fact is, I began to take more time off work and enjoy the time I now had with my family.

Michele and I have written this book with the intent to influence you to read <u>Becoming Your Own Banker</u> by R.

Nelson Nash. We are fully aware of many other books written on this topic and it is not our intent to augment or replace those other works. Our aim is to provide an avenue which allows you to comprehend and command the power you have over you own finances.

Exposing the Mystique Surrounding Money

Chapter One

A lie told often enough becomes the truth. – *Vladimir Lenin*

Bankers have been known throughout the centuries as those who know money. Originally bankers were nothing more than warehouse owners who stored gold, or other precious metals, for others and charged a fee for doing so. Later these warehousemen became money changers as they facilitated exchange permitting their security notes, issued for the stored commodity, to be signed over to another owner without the original owner physically cashing in the note. This allowed the owner of the stored gold to use their security notes for trade--- the purchase of goods and services--- and the new owner of the note would be guaranteed redemption rights to the stored gold.

As many of these warehousemen were goldsmiths, it followed that the goldsmiths were left holding large amounts of inventory---gold and precious metals. And therefore, dishonest goldsmiths could issue more security notes (notes in excess of what they really had stored in their warehouse.)

Realizing that the probability of all depositors demanding their physical gold simultaneously was relatively low, these dishonest goldsmiths found that they profited by supplying themselves, or their close friends and business associates, with excessive notes. And though this profit was illicit it didn't keep some goldsmiths, turned bankers, from participating in this dishonest practice.

Of course this practice put more notes into circulation than there was in actual reserves (stored gold and precious metals.) And the first to feel the effects of this increased money supply were the merchants. The merchants necessarily had to pass this increased cost of doing business directly on to their consumers in the form of higher consumer prices. And consumer inflation was born.

Higher consumer prices have historically been referred to as inflation but in reality inflation is the dishonest practice of bankers who produce fiat currency (paper money or electronic money in today's economy) without having adequate reserves to back it up. This practice is also called monetizing (or of late, quantitative easing... QE) and it is still practiced today by literally all centralized banks throughout the world. This dishonest practice is what has given bankers a bad name. It is also what has caused the American dollar to lose 95% of its purchasing power since 1913.

Why 1913? Because that was when this practice of dishonest banking became legal---legal at least for an elite group who now hold the monopoly on the printing (creating) of money in the United States--- but certainly not honest. These elite few are now empowered to create money out of thin air by the United States Congress under the Federal Reserve Act which President Wilson signed into law in 1913.

As mentioned earlier, consumers call the side effects of this process inflation tending to believe political and social opportunists who blame merchants for being greedy. But in reality inflation is the creation of money (paper or electronic) which is not based on any real tangible reserves.

Examine any United States paper money that you currently have in your possession. Read what it is called---it is called a Federal Reserve Note. This note is the legal tender of the United States. But just because it is legal doesn't make it just, honest or even accurate. To be just, honest and accurate it would have to be precise and that would mean; for every Federal Reserve Note that exists (or for every electronic Federal Reserve Note that is accounted for) there would have to be a corresponding amount of reserves (precious metals) owned or stored by the Federal Reserve or the system that it controls. Because that isn't the case, the green piece of paper held in your possession currently is worthless except that it has been classified as legal tender.

Real inflation; therefore, has really nothing to do with greedy merchants and everything to do with greedy and dishonest practices of politicians, social engineers and central bankers... like the Federal Reserve.

Because of this fact, inflation has become the most insidious and subtle way to make (steal) money. In reality inflation is the transfer of wealth from an unknowing group of people to a very select few who happen to control the printing presses (or computers) which produce all legal tender. This dishonesty, though completely "*legal*" today, is destroying the economic matrix of our country and our world. The people who control and benefit from this inflationary process are subject to the same judgment which was pronounced many years ago on certain money changers of that day.

- "When He saw what the money changers were doing, He was incensed and He made a scourge (or whip) and drove the bankers out of the Temple by force and destroyed their tables, along with their records, receipts, etc."[4,5]

Why would a teacher of peace, resort to such physical measures? The answer is very simple: The Teacher here saw the reality of what was happening... inflation in action! And inflation is an unfair weight and an unjust measure! As such, it is the most insidious form of slavery which has ever been contrived and/or practiced throughout history. It allows men and women to think that they are free while in reality they become more and more enslaved to time and wages. The harder and longer they work, the more their time belongs to someone else beside themselves. Every minute which they have been blessed with, when converted and limited to the wages they can earn, is just one more minute of their life that has been stolen from them. And all by the inflationary process described previously. Inflation creates a perpetually evolving, never ending system of bondage in which the worker, producer, and consumer become further and further subjected to their hidden masters--- the bankers, politicians and social engineers who own or control the process that "creates" money out of thin air. Historically inflationary slavery leads to social unrest, violence against other people's personal property and mob rule witnessed as recently as in modern day Greece.

Our excellent team members here at Life Benefits, Inc. will be delighted to serve you! So go ahead, pick up the phone and make that call 1-866-502-2777 or you can email us: team@life-benefits.com

----

[4] Chuck Baldwin, February 26, 2008; NewsWithViews.com
[5] John 2:14,15

Banking: An Essential of a Thriving Economy

Chapter Two

A half-truth is often a great lie. ---*Anonymous*

"There is no free lunch" quipped the late Economist Milton Friedman. Friedman was right---at least on this point. There is no free lunch. And this holds true with banking as well as with anything else. Would you expect a warehouse to store your personal goods for free? Neither did traders, merchants and consumers of days gone by. When they stored their precious currencies---gold and silver---they expected to pay a fee for that service. Furthermore, they expected that their property would be protected or "insured" so that when they submitted their security note their goods would be returned to them in their entirety.

This fee naturally had to be an agreed upon fee, worthy and honest. It was largely dependent upon the integrity of the banker and his ability to keep the goods entrusted to him in safe keeping until the day or hour which the owner came to reclaim them. No doubt, an honest banker with an excellent reputation would have been able to ask and receive a higher fee for this service than a dishonest banker who was known to fabricate notes or who squandered the deposits entrusted to his keeping.

In much the same way that you or I would little afford to work for free or without some form of compensation---the honest banker could ill afford to provide safe keeping of other's goods without a service fee. But as banking evolved, an even more profitable way to encourage people to deposit with them was discovered by bankers. Instead of charging their depositors more for the storage fee---they began to pay depositors a small percentage in exchange for the right to loan out the stored commodities (or notes on those commodities) to others. When the bankers did this they charged the borrowers (the risk takers) a fee for use of this money.

This was a capital concept! It afforded you-the-depositor an opportunity to earn a profit while storing your commodities. At the same time it kept your commodity in circulation. This circulation kept the cost of goods and services relatively stable throughout the economy. At the same time it also encouraged entrepreneurs to borrow these "new" available assets---assuming the risk that they could make the payments on the borrowed assets---and produce a higher profit by expanding their ability to provide more goods and services to you-the-consumer. The increased goods and services provided from this turn of events resulted in lower prices and better selection of goods and service for the entire community. Capitalism was born and the world became a wealthier place for all to live and function in because of it. (For further information concerning this concept refer to The Mystery of Banking by Murray Rothbard.)

Through this process the idea of "your money working for you" was born. Bankers were now in the business of lending money as well as in the business of storing money. This provided a rate of return to those who stored their capital with the bankers. Of course, the bankers earned more this way too as they were able to charge the borrower a rate which was in relation to the risk taken and they passed the true risk off to the owner of the stored commodity.

This entire process increased the circulation of money in society which beforehand had been "horded"... locked up in storage. Up until this time in history wealth consisted almost entirely of inventories---inventories which were in actuality a liability to their owners because there was a cost in protecting and/or preventing their being lost, stolen or destroyed.

In becoming the lender of other people's money bankers indemnified the risk associated with this lending by making the owners of the capital being lent liable for any loss. Bankers astutely never assumed that risk themselves. By positioning themselves in this manner a banker's profits are as near to being guaranteed as possible because the risk has been shifted back to the depositor.

This process, which we refer to as the "banking equation," creates a high profit for the banker through the use (flow) of money, without risk to the banker. This profit is often misclassified as usury. But in reality this profit is no different than you or me being paid for a job fulfilled. You or I exchange our time, skills, services and expertise for money and the banker exchanges his time, skills, services and expertise for money. The idea of money being used to make money has nothing to do with the negative, almost slanderous, term called usury---unless of course there is dishonesty involved.

In reality this profit is an honest wage earned for an honest service rendered and is properly called profit... interest profit to be exact. Interest earned in this way is the rightful wage of any honest banker. The problem arises when the banker creates more "notes" than what he actually has on reserve (stored) and lends or spends those notes as if they were backed 100% by real capital. When this happens capitalism is given a black eye or dishonestly blamed

7

because the inflationary practices of the banker are concealed to most. And because they are concealed the masses tend to blame the "greedy" merchant (capitalist) who must raise the prices on goods and services because his money has lost its value. The only other choice is to go out of business and then there would be less goods and services for everybody.

Therefore, simply said, bankers who lend out more money than what they have stored in their vaults are fraudulent. The interest which they earn on these fraudulent notes, created out of thin air, **becomes usury** because usury uses and abuses innocent people who have placed their trust in bankers. These trusting souls; therefore, inadvertently become slaves to the bankers simply because of their trusting nature. As mentioned before, inflationary practices produce higher prices for everybody in society. Only the creators of this *"funny money"* reap advantage from it. Is it any wonder that true religion historically has always banned the practice of usury? This is because usury, through its inflationary practices, destroys the very society in which we must all exist and thrive. It creates a master race, a group of elitists who enslave the rest of the world for their own dishonest and self-serving purposes.

However, aside from the downright fraudulent money creation and usury practices of these dishonest bankers, there are other common practices, which although they may not be completely dishonest are packaged in such a way as to appear better than they actually are. For an example of this consider when a banker behaves like a borrower and promises… guarantees… an average annual rate of return (ARR.) To most folks an ARR implies that the depositor (investor) will actually earn the stated rate on the principal he/she invests or deposits. But upon closer examination, rates of return can turn out much differently than what the average depositor/investor might first believe.

A guaranteed rate of return on a specific deposit/investment, a banker may tell you---even guarantee you in writing--- will produce a 15% return over a course of say 4 years. But when the actual results are in, you may lose money on the deal--- and that even before you pay taxes!

How is this possible, you might be asking?

Simple, rate of return is not the same thing as yield. Rate of return is an average of the gains and losses over a specified period of time. It doesn't reflect real profits---or losses for that matter. Yield, on the other hand, is exactly what it implies---a profit or an actual gain which is *retained* on the original principal deposited or invested.

In the book <u>A Path to Financial Peace of Mind</u> the author brilliantly explains that the "Average rate of return is not the same as compound interest..." The sad truth is that at the end of a four-year period, you will likely have less than what you started with because along the way there have been sales charges, fees, and other expenses. The point is that the average rate of return is not as important to you as the amount of money in your account. What do you care if your fund boasts a 10%, 15%, or 25% rate of return if your cash balance is not increasing? In reality the return of your money is more important than the rate of return on your money.

Let me make it clear that the legality of a banker guaranteeing a certain rate of return is not in question here, but what about honesty? Yield is not the same thing as rate of return! To guarantee to someone that they will profit

10% or 15% is not the same thing as a guaranteed rate of return of 10% or 15%. But bankers are allowed, even encouraged, to do "this" in a society which today ironically prides itself on being so legally and politically correct---- legal only because of all the fanciful laws that have been socially engineered but certainly not just and honest, as too many have been duped to believe.

This same concept holds true when you consider the other side of the equation in the banking industry---the lending side---and annual percentage rates (APR.) APR is only one portion of a formula which must be known in its entirety to fully comprehend the consequences of any loan.

Contemplate this, if you will...purchase a house at $250,000 with an APR of 5% on a 30 year term mortgage. You WILL end up paying more than 5% of your total payments in interest over the next 30 years. Fact is, you'll end up paying closer to 50% of your total payments in interest---if you keep the house for the full 30 years and never refinance it. If you refinance it, that total cost of interest will go up--- even if you refinance at a lower rate!

How can this be? The math tells the honest truth.

- With a 5% APR the monthly payment will be $1,342.05 per month.
- Pay $1,342.05 x 360 months (30 years) and you'll pay $483,139.46 for your $250,000 house.
- That means that $233,139.46 of all your payments went to pay interest.
- That's roughly 48%. 48% is not 5%.
- 5% is only the annual rate at which you paid the interest.

Volume of Interest
$250k Mortgage, 5% APR, 30 Years

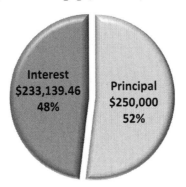

The entire equation is *Interest = Principal x Rate/Time Period* applied for each period of time during the term of the loan.

- APR is only one portion of that entire equation and tells you nothing of importance by itself.
- Refinance your house in 5 years and you will have paid $80,523.24 to the mortgage company but $60,095.11 of those dollars will have been interest!
- That means you have now paid 75% interest.
- Repeat this process every 5 years like the average American does and you've only compounded your interest payments to the mortgage company.

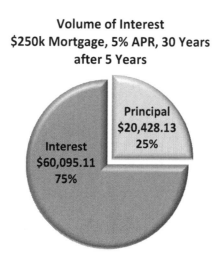

Volume of Interest
$250k Mortgage, 5% APR, 30 Years
after 5 Years

Principal
$20,428.13
25%

Interest
$60,095.11
75%

So what about interest only loans? Why does everyone tell you not to take out an interest only loan? Don't they tell you that all your payments will be interest and no principal?

Well, once again let's explore some fundamental mathematical facts and see what is really going on.

- That same 30 year, $250,000 mortgage at 5%, if it was an interest only mortgage would require you to pay only the interest on the principal balance each month with a final principal payment of $250,000.
- Therefore an interest only loan provides more flexibility for you as the borrower than a normal principal and interest loan does.
- This is because the required monthly payment is less... requiring only the interest.
- Therefore the interest only loan provides you the borrower with an extra option, namely to satisfy just

the interest on the loan while keeping your principal working for you somewhere else besides sitting uselessly as equity in your house.

- As with anything else in life it all comes down to discipline. Obviously you must be responsible when managing the principal yourself.

Why then aren't interest only loans more common? Perhaps people don't like the responsibility. Or maybe the general population hasn't educated themselves enough to understand the simple math necessary to understand this process? Maybe the government schooling system hasn't taught the general public enough to understand this math? Maybe bankers want to use this equity themselves? Maybe, maybe, maybe...? Who really knows or cares? But the absolute truth is this; an interest only loan, managed intelligently, is a powerful and profitable tool in the hands of the borrower. Only someone who is ignorant or a liar will attempt to bamboozle you with a different story line.

So how does an honest banker make a profit, you might ask?

And the simple answer would be: By disclosing all the facts about annual rates of returns, annual percentage rates, interest only loans and the like. That being done thoroughly, a person who is considering using their services would understand what is really going on. And when that happens people are intelligent enough to make an informed and educated decision about whether they need the services of the bank or not. If they do, then an honest banker will earn his due profits. If not, the profits will go elsewhere because there will be a profit made when money flows and the one who's the banker of the deal will always be the one who will glean the most profit. It; therefore, becomes paramount for you to learn, to think and to behave like an honest banker.

The chief objective of this entire book is to confirm that you can learn to think and behave like an honest banker! And when you do, the services of conventional banks are no longer necessary---except for the convenience they provide like checking accounts and credit cards. That's right! The grandest deception which has been perpetrated upon society today by the social engineers, bankers and politicians is that everybody has to use conventional banks. Everybody has been taught to believe there is no other option! That is a hoax!

Our team here at Life Benefits, Inc. is dedicated to helping you achieve your goals. Call our office and become the honest "banker" in your life. 1-866-502-2777 or email: team@life-benefits.com

The Solution

Chapter Three

Most of the basic truths of life sound absurd at first hearing. - Elizabeth Goudge

The more you think and behave like an honest banker the more money you will have to work with! Nothing wrong with that, is there? Really, there is no limit to your wealth because your wealth will no longer just be found stored in some inventory (i.e., CD's, stocks, bonds, money market accounts, real estate, pension plans, qualified plans, etc.) No, your true wealth will become something you create yourself. And it will be limited only by your own imagination.

My friend and mentor always told me, "Tom, there are only three types of wealth in the world:

1) Wealth that comes from your heritage; your family, your genetic makeup.
2) Wealth that comes from what you've learned; your experiences, what others have taught you and what the Spirit of God has shared with you.
3) Wealth that consists of things; things you can touch, taste, feel, and own---material things and money."

I would like to make one addition to that list... freedom. Freedom is also wealth... it is the liberty to behave in accordance to your own beliefs, thoughts and imaginations without harming another's wealth or station in life.

Freedom is a form of personal authority, clout, influence and persuasion. In a word freedom is power!

Now if you had to relinquish one of these four types of wealth, which type of wealth would you give up?

If you are willing to give up anything other than the third type of wealth, then this book is probably not for you. Please just pass it on to someone else who might benefit from it instead, because all the other types of wealth are irreplaceable.

However, if you would be willing to give up the third type of wealth, in order to retain the remaining three, then you've already come to realize that the third type of wealth is a by-product of the other three. Take the other three forms of wealth away from an individual, a community, a country or the world and there will be massive slavery, poverty and wretchedness. There is no other alternative. Protect and nourish the rights to possess and control the three remaining forms of wealth in a family, a society or an individual and there will be so much production (wealth) that the entire world will become a better, cleaner, more affluent place in which all humanity can live and thrive.

This is, in essence, the American experiment! No nation in the entire history of the world had ever been able to produce as much wealth as America did throughout the 19th and 20th centuries. That was when America held these three forms of wealth as sacred rights of all individuals. Sadly, we have entered an era where these basic forms of liberty are being vilified, ignored and stolen from the individual via government regulation, oppressive oversight and blatant disregard of the truth, knowledge and wisdom that have been passed down for centuries from generation to generation. Sir Isaac Newton, the great mathematical genius, was fully aware that his genius was not his own when he stated that "this generation can only stand as tall as it can reach by standing on the shoulders of the previous generation." This generation needs to consider that they are creating less for their children and grandchildren because they have not held these three forms of wealth as inalienable rights belonging to all. Thomas Jefferson plainly warned us that our "Democracy will cease to exist when you take away from those who are willing to work and give to those who will not."

Now consider how honest bankers were vilified in thirteenth century England. Note what history documents concerning that society and what it turned into over the next several centuries. Think it can't happen here in America? Think again. If dishonest laws and regulations continue to pile up encumbering and inconveniencing the practice of honest banking in our society, then we can expect the same thing or worse to happen here in America as well. You see "King Edward saw himself able to conciliate powerful elements and escape from awkward debts, by the simple and well-trodden path of anti-Semitism... The Jews were held up to universal hatred, were pillaged, maltreated and finally expelled from the realm..! Not until four centuries had elapsed was Oliver Cromwell, by furtive contact with a moneyed Israelite, able to open again the coast of England to the enterprise of the Jewish race."[6] Federal regulations on commerce, political correctness and so called "anti-terrorism" policies, in many ways, have become blatant bigotry. Bigotry is dishonest. It always favors one person, group or class above another. Such favoritism is not the practice of "liberty and justice for all" and therefore will produce the same poverty and wretchedness that it historically has shown to always

---

[6] Winston Churchill

17

produce. The laws of nature cannot be ignored without suffering the consequences.

So what can be done?

It is paramount that individuals begin to listen and regard the wisdom which our forefathers gleaned and passed on to us... the basic concept surrounding personal freedom which allows individuals to produce and profit without undue regulation, persecution or harassment! Otherwise these freedoms will continue to be damaged, denigrated and ultimately demolished which can only lead to poverty and wretchedness for individuals and society in general, demoralizing and destroying the world as we know it today.

Frankly, this task of is an individual responsibility and not a government job. Too many people involved in government are part of the problem already; and therefore, have excluded themselves from being a part of the real solution. No, the effort must begin at the "you and me level" as Leonard Read so eloquently spoke years ago. This is because an idea prepared in a mind, will only reach another mind, but an idea lived will reach another life. And one life at a time the truth will overpower a world of minds! This is because a life can only be shared in a relationship and relationships are always at the "you and me level."

So how does any of this apply to thinking and behaving like an honest banker? Hang on, we're almost there.

The Process

Chapter Four

The best mind-altering drug is truth. - Lily Tomlin

What if you knew about a place where you could store your money, earn a guaranteed yield on it and still be able to use your money at the same time...without any penalties... no fees and no services charges?

What if you knew that you could use your money to make it grow more money and that when your money grew it wouldn't face any further taxes on the growth?

What if you could continue to use the growth of your money and by using it the only down side would be that you'd have more money to use?

What if you could do all this and still have no debt? No creditors? No liabilities?

What if you were told this secure and safe place to grow your money has been around for over 200 years and that it is used by thousands of people, business owners, corporations and bankers daily?

What if it were known to you that the process to accomplish all this was very simple and easy to access?

What emotions would you experience realizing that nobody had ever taken the time to tell you about this?

What else would you want to know about this process?

What time would you think it best to learn more about this process?

What kind of money could you afford to put to work in such a system?

Well, if you weren't too thrilled about any of the "whats" mentioned above then stop! Don't read any further. Just pass this book along to somebody else that might benefit from what I'm about to share next. Because if you didn't get excited over any of those "whats" then you're most likely indifferent to creating a happier, healthier, wealthier environment for yourself while blessing your posterity to boot. So please, save yourself the trouble of reading more. I promise you it won't benefit you in the least.

If, on the contrary, your curiosity was even slightly piqued then read on because what I'm about to share is one of the most exciting things in the world of finance that most have never even heard about. And all I'm going to share with you is how to think and behave like an honest banker.

Right now when you earn or receive money you most likely put that money into someone else's bank. That allows the banker to loan your money out to others, but it limits you the use of your own money. For sure you can withdraw it, write a check against it, debit it, etc. until it's all gone, but you can't really use your money and still earn interest on it while you use it. *Only a banker can loan your money out and still make money on your money while it's being used.* By lending (depositing) your money to the bank you have limited your ability to use your own money. Let me repeat myself. You can still: 1) withdraw it, 2) write a check on it (same effect as withdrawing it,) 3) use a debit card (same effect as withdrawing it,) or 4) leave it on loan (deposit) at the bank and earn whatever interest the banker will give you. And what the banker does pay you will be considered taxable income.

But take your money and deposit it (pay a premium) into a participating whole life insurance policy that is properly designed for your financial needs (instead of paying more commissions to an insurance agent by purchasing a higher death benefit,) and things change dramatically in your favor!

- First of all, the premiums paid into a participating whole life insurance policy have guaranteed cash values that are promised throughout the life of the policy contract.

- Secondly, because this is guaranteed cash value, not an investment or rate of return, the growth is not subject to the volatility of the market or fluctuating interest rates.

- Thirdly, cash value growth is not considered taxable income under current IRS code.

- Fourthly, part of this growth (dividends) can be used to increase the face value of your life insurance policy which is the legacy you are building to pass on to the next generation.

- Fifth and finally, as you put the money available in the cash values to work for you, the company can still pay you dividends on your policy. Again these dividends are not taxable under the current Internal Revenue Code, as long as they are not withdrawn but are used to purchase more face value in the policy.

Now comes the good part!

Because you now own an asset (life insurance with a face value[7] and a cash value[8]) you are now guaranteed by the company you purchased that asset from, that you can become the borrower of the funds which the company has to lend out in order for your death benefit[9] to be paid someday in the future. The only questions the company will ever ask you when you go to borrow this cash value are this. "How much have you paid in and how much have you taken out already? Isn't this the same thing any money lender needs to know when you borrow, use your debit card or withdraw money from your conventional accounts today?

When you ask for this money you can either ask to withdraw money or you can just borrow money from the insurance company. If you withdraw your money from your policy it's just like when you withdraw money from your conventional bank account or investment... the growth is forfeited on the amount that you withdraw because you stop earning interest on the amount of money you've taken out. If, however, you ask for a loan instead of a withdrawal the company will loan it to you and use the face value in your policy as collateral. In this way you will continue to earn the guaranteed return paid by the life insurance company on your policy with no penalties!

---

[7] Face Value: The total amount of money the policy will be worth upon your death.

[8] Cash Value: The dollar amount of money that the insurance company will loan you based upon your face value.

[9] Death Benefit: The total amount of money that the company will pay your beneficiaries upon your death.

Now you're starting to think like an honest banker, but you'll also need to behave like one or you'll soon part with your money and your ability to create wealth with it! So let's go back to the classroom of life for a review of some basic mathematics.

In 1998 I started saving (paying myself) $500 per month. The purpose of this savings account was the need of a different vehicle. I had been taught to purchase everything by paying cash for it. So I had to pay myself first to make that happen. By the year 2000 I'd saved up $10,000, which at that time was earning 4% in a CD. Sadly, I knew nothing about behaving like an honest banker back then. So I withdrew my $10,000 and purchased a vehicle for my family feeling very pleased with myself for not incurring any debt!

I cried then, and still cringe, over this and other purchases I've made throughout my life time exactly in this same manner...our home, our business, all of our possessions, our vacations, our daily living expenses...! Why did I cry? Because I realized for the first time in my life how much money I had lost because I paid cash for everything. Instead of the financial freedom I'd been taught paying cash was, I realized that paying cash was yet another form of financial slavery which innocent people had bought into, and I had been gullible enough to believe it all... without checking it out thoroughly enough to know the difference!

And here's the reason why. When I paid cash for our home that was when the roof started leaking. All my savings had gone to purchase the house so what was left for me to do? I worked harder so I could afford to fix the roof. When I paid cash for my cars, my savings went to purchase the cars, so when the kids needed clothes I worked harder and longer hours to make the money needed to buy their clothes. When I paid cash for the business expenses, I didn't have any money left to pay payroll, so I worked longer and harder to make sure I could meet payroll obligations...!

Now don't get me wrong, we all have expenses and necessities in life. But what I'm pointing out is this--- paying cash for everything and being debt free isn't the financial freedom that you have been told it is. I know. I lived that lifestyle for 45 long years! And that was before today's popular prophets had learned to profit off you by charging your credit card for their program and then telling you to cut those same cards up and live on what you make, paying cash for everything, renting until you can own, etc., etc. That lifestyle does not produce financial freedom. Matter of fact that kind of lifestyle produces burnout and bondage!

Think about this for a moment. Is it your burning desire to work longer and harder for every new pleasure or expense that comes along in your life? What about every vacation you want to take? Perhaps every gift you fancy to purchase for a loved one? Maybe all the charity you'd like to share with those less fortunate than yourself? Do you want to continually work harder and longer for all these things in your life?

Or perhaps you realize how much more straightforward and productive it would be if you were able to use your own money for the things that you need in life and by doing so produce a profit that would enable you to do all the other things that you long and desire to accomplish as well?

That is what thinking and behaving like an honest banker can provide for you... freedom to be more productive, more charitable, healthy and; therefore, without having to work harder or longer, more wealthy. The only other option is to trade your time for wages and become more and more enslaved to the clock, so that you can afford to do the things you want to do in life.

So examine the reasons why I lost so much of my wealth when I insisted on paying cash for everything throughout the first 45 years of my life.

When I took my $10,000 and withdrew it from where it was earning 4% to buy the vehicle in 2000, I stopped earning the 4% profit on that money. This means, that on that $10,000 withdrawal alone, I lost $831.43 of pure interest profit over the next 24 months.

Interest lost on $10,000 at 4% for 2 years = $831.43

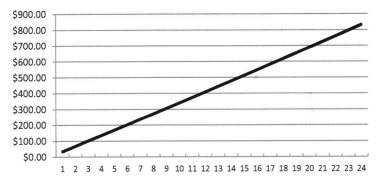

Now I could have borrowed the needed $10,000 at that time for only 6%. And over the next 24 months I would have only had to pay the banker $443.21 per month for that loan. But this is where I knew I must lose money. How can you borrow money at a higher rate (6%) than what you're saving money at (4%) and not lose money?

Well, when you pay interest to someone else you do lose money no question about it. The interest you pay is lost, gone forever, because it goes to someone else as their just and honest wage which they deserve for providing you the opportunity to use their money.

But what happens if you can keep your money working for you while you are paying someone else for the use of their money? The answer is... you can limit your loss. In this specific scenario the profit you earn from your own money at work will offset the cost of what you are paying in interest to someone else for the use of their money. At the end of the day the cost difference can be completely nullified for you. That is, you can actually earn a profit yourself if you are astute.

This is what I learned about my $10,000 vehicle purchase. If I were to have kept my money where it was earning 4% interest for 24 months, the interest earned would have compounded in my favor and I would have earned $831.43.

Interest gained on $10,000 at 4% for 2 years = $831.43

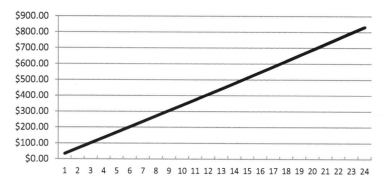

Granted, I then would have had to borrow someone else's money to purchase the vehicle because we still needed that vehicle. But the borrowed money (at 6%) would have only cost me $636.95 of interest over the same 24 month period time.

Interest paid on $10,000 loan at 6% for 2 years = $636.95

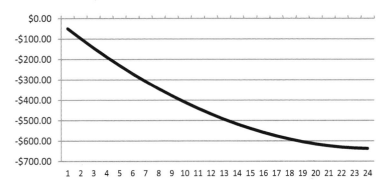

That means that I would have still cleared (profited) $194.48.[10] But I had always been told I would lose 2% (4% - 6% = -2% right?) Not so when you do the math and consider the time factor in the banking equation! That is how bankers behave. Because bankers have a more complete understanding of how money really works, bankers never confuse numbers with money.

---

[10] Another option is to withdraw and use the $10,000 that was earning 4% and make payments of $443.21 back into the account earning 4% instead of making payments to a third party lender at 6%. This option would be more profitable $417.99 vs. $194.48, but would exclude the benefits of owning participating whole life insurance in conjunction with financing your life needs.

Difference of saving $10,000 at 4% while borrowing at 6% over 2 years = $194.48

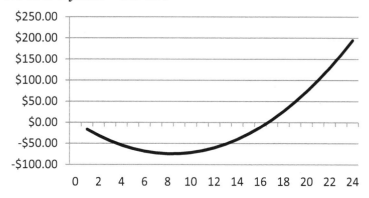

Think about this for a moment. Bankers always make more money when interest rates are low, but most everybody else seems to think that bankers make more money when interest rates are high. The reason for this is very straightforward: When rates are low bankers don't have to pay as much to their depositors to get them to deposit money with them. Yet when someone borrows money from the banker the banker may charge them double the rate (or more) over and beyond what he pays his depositors. For example, if you deposit money in a bank and profit 1% on it and the banker can charge me 2% to borrow that money, then the banker makes a 100% profit! He takes in 2% and keeps half and gives you the other half. But when rates rise and he now has to pay you 3% for your deposited money he may only be able to get 5% from me when I borrow it from him. Now the banker can only keep 2% of the 5% he charged me because he has to give 3% back to you. His profit has dropped from 100% to only 66.67%! Do you understand more about interest rates now and why central bankers try to keep interest rates low?

But getting back to my vehicle purchase and how you can learn to behave like an honest banker. What would have happened if I would have had $10,000 of cash value in a participating whole life insurance policy instead of a commercial bank? I could have asked the insurance company for a loan of $10,000 and purchased my vehicle with that borrowed money. The insurance company would have used my policy's face value as collateral on the $10,000 loan and I would have been able to continue to earn the returns, plus any dividends, which the policy contractually provided me without paying any penalties or losing any guarantees.

Of course, I would want to pay the insurance company back for the loan, and the least complicated way for me to do that would have been to pay them what I would have had to pay the commercial bank for the same loan...$443.21 a month for 24 months. (By the way $443.21 is $56.79 less than the $500 I was comfortable paying to myself per month when I was saving up that $10,000 in the first place. This whole process just gets better if I would continue to pay back what I had been used to paying myself...the $500 per month...instead of only $443.21 which the conventional bank would have charged.) But at $443.21 per month, by the end of 24 months, I would now have $636.95 of interest that normally would have gone to the commercial bank working for me instead of being lost to the commercial bank. (This interest wouldn't actually be in my pocket but would have been paid to the insurance company and because I am a participating policy owner of the mutual company the money would be working for me.) On top of that I would still have earned the $831.43.[11]

---

[11] For illustrative purposes the same numbers are used here as in the pure compounding interest example; however, most insurance

So how can the $636.95 of interest that I paid back to the insurance company still work for me if I had to pay that interest to the insurance company? There is a straightforward answer to that question once you understand participating whole life insurance, how it is designed and how it functions.

You see, when you take a loan from an insurance company against your participating whole life policy, the company holds your face value as collateral for that loan. The company doesn't take money out of your policy unless you withdraw money from your policy. Money loaned to you comes from the general fund of the insurance company. If you decide not to pay the loan back (or die before you pay the loan back) then the insurance company will deduct from your face value the amount of interest and principal that you owe them and the rest will go to your beneficiary(s.)

On the other hand, if you pay the insurance company back along with the interest that they charged you for the loan there will be no decrease in your face value. If you pay them back extra interest then your face value will grow. And as your face value increases so does the value of your cash value (i.e., the amount of money the insurance company can loan to you on request.) That is the way a participating whole life policy works.

So, in my personal example of the vehicle purchase, if I would have purchased the vehicle with a participating

---

companies compound policy loan interest on an annual vs. monthly basis and guaranteed policy values do not compound at a direct rate of interest, but also factor in mortality and general operating expenses of the company.

whole life insurance loan and paid back to the insurance company what I would have had to pay to the commercial bank. Then I would have had:

- The vehicle
- The guaranteed cash value increase in my policy
- The interest I would have paid to someone else to use their money now working for me
- And a face value (death benefit) in a life insurance policy to protect and benefit my loved ones or charity

Instead, when I paid cash for the vehicle, even though I had the vehicle, I lost. I lost:

- The money that my money could have made
- The money that I could have paid myself via the policy loan repayment
- The death benefit that my family would now be guaranteed of if I had paid premium with my $10,000

Our coaches at Life Benefits, Inc. are licensed insurance agents, we custom design and sell you the product that best fits your needs. Then we're also here to coach you as you make those "what ifs" in your life come true.

Call our office 1-866-502-2777 or email us: team@life-benefits.com

The Reason Why

Chapter Five

*Speaking the truth in times of universal deceit is a
revolutionary behavior.* - George Orwell

Now in a somewhat contrary way to everything I've said up
to this point, behaving like an honest banker will not make
you a wealthy person. That is because wealth is a created
entity. Wealth flows from above down, inside to outside
just like life, health and faith. Wealth is vitalistic not
mechanistic. As Rabbi Daniel Lapin says, "money is
spiritual." There is no magic spell, incantation or sacred
rite which you can ascribe to or recite ritually in order to
become wealthy (this in spite of what one author writes---
whose claim is to reveal the millionaire's mind---) that
"wealth only makes you more of what you already are."

This, at best, is only a half-truth because you first have to
become a new person in order to create new wealth.
Otherwise you will only attempt, with various results, to
accumulate the wealth which others have created. The old
axiom of putting new wine into old wineskins is
appropriate here. The old wine skin will burst and you will
ruin both the old skin and the new wine if you attempt to
fill yourself up with wealth and not alter yourself to receive
that wealth. The only place to put new wine is in a new
wine skin. You can't expect an old wine skin to adequately
accept and control the fermentation process that new wine
will produce.

The same is true of wealth, you have to become a new you
in order to produce or create new wealth. You can't just
become more of what you already are or you'll destroy

33

yourself in the process. But the wonder of it all is this: When you learn to become a new and better person you'll automatically begin to create and produce new wealth. This wealth is the wealth that only you are capable of producing. Furthermore, this wealth which emanates from you is unique because of who you are and what you are becoming, something nobody else can emulate or reproduce.

So, in order to create real wealth you must, by necessity, become a new you! Not just more of what you already are. Even though seeds of your potential wealth are definitely within you from the beginning it is up to you to cultivate, water and fertilize them in order for your growth to occur. So yes, you do have the seeds for wealth genetically implanted inside you, but you will have to nurture them in order for them to grow or nothing spectacular will ever happen to those seeds.

With this thought in mind, thinking and behaving like an honest banker isn't like an MLM because it doesn't depend on your down-line, up-line or any other person to make it happen. It isn't like trading equities, securities, money markets, real estate or even like managing a business. Thinking and behaving like an honest banker is different than any type of investing mentionable because the process isn't an investment at all. Investments inherently require you to assume an unknown risk. But thinking and behaving like an honest banker doesn't require you to assume anything. In fact, when you think and behave like an honest banker you are planning for a **known risk**...death.

Now something that is as sure as death **can** be planned for even though it can't be avoided. Something that is unknown never can be fully planned for or avoided. So why assume the risk of investments? You see, you can either plan around what you know for sure will happen...death; or you can gamble about what you think might happen...the unknown future. It's your choice.

The bottom line is this: You know yourself better than anybody else in the world. Can you trust yourself enough to plan for your own future? That in a nut shell is what it takes to be able to think and to behave like an honest banker. Nothing else is required...even the insurance policy that you will utilize in this exercise of thinking and behaving like an honest banker has already been designed for you. The insurance company's actuaries have done all that work for you. All that is necessary for you to do is find yourself a good coach who is qualified to help you fine tune one of those policies into a contract which will work in your best interests. And those interests should be the self-financing of your future acquisitions in life.

Speaking of your coach: You must doubly make sure that your coach is someone who has been thinking and behaving like an honest banker himself! If you fail to do so you may end up like too many folks I've run into---thinking the insurance company is going to make all this happen for you. It's not the insurance company, nor is it your financial planner, or for that matter your CPA, who's going to make this work for you. No, it will be entirely up to you and your coach. The two of you will become the most important players in the whole game. And ultimately it's going to boil down to you! It is you that will make the ultimate difference! Remember, I said you'll have to become a new you.

So, secure for yourself a knowledgeable, capable and experienced coach.[12] In doing so you'll learn to perform at your ultimate potential. Isn't that what having a coach is all about, helping you realize and perform to your fullest potential? But be very conscious of this fact; no coach, however experienced, capable or knowledgeable, will ever be able to help you do what you cannot and do not want to do for yourself. You have to provide the desire!

Now desire is not just some wishful dreaming about what you need, want or expect. Desire is a yearning or longing that stirs you so deeply that you're compelled to either take action or burst. When you have this kind of passion along with good coaching you'll surpass even your own remotest imaginings. And what other imaginings besides your own would you like to surpass? Wasn't it Shakespeare who exhorted us all by saying, "To thine own self be true."

To take ownership of this type of passion you must be certain that wealth is not an evil any more than poverty is a virtue. Money often can become the focus of evil or dishonest minds if the other forms of wealth discussed in chapter three are not held in sacred honor. But wealth which is created through the exercise of the moral good which was implanted in you at birth can never be classified as an evil in and of itself. Wealth so created is a blessing. To view it as anything otherwise is an evil---a curse in the face of God who placed those seeds of wealth in you from the beginning. Furthermore, for you not to cultivate these internal seeds of wealth, with the full intent of growing them to their completest potential, creates blight, poverty---

---

[12] Life Benefits, Inc. and "Your Wealth Team" are a seasoned group of coaches who own their own participating whole life insurance policies and have used them personally to self-finance things in their own life and now coach hundreds of others around the globe how to do the same.

less wealth---for all Creation because those seeds were provided to you according to your ability and were intended to bless and enrich your life as well as the lives of everybody around you! If you hoard and amass the seeds of wealth entrusted to you without properly cultivating them to full maturation they will rot and perish turning what was meant for a blessing into an interminable loss or curse to all mankind, not the least of whom is you.

So realize what potential profit already resides within you just waiting to thrive and blossom. This will ignite your passion. And not just a passion for money but a passion to redeem your time, your thoughts, your relationships, and your life... real and lasting wealth! Remember, you are not a wage slave but a free man! Begin to behave and think accordingly. Your wealth is at stake.

They are like trees that grow beside a stream, that bear fruit at the right time, and whose leaves do not dry up. They succeed in everything they do. --- Psalms 1:3

Do you have the desire to succeed? I thought so. Here at Life Benefits, Inc. we all agree that is a noble desire, so of course we're here to help you. Call our office 1-866-502-2777 or email us: team@life-benefits.com

Value of Protection

Chapter Six

You can only find truth with logic if you have already found truth without it. - G. K. Chesterton

There's a reason why this chapter is number six and not number one. Like Chesterton implied, logic is only helpful to those who have already discovered truth. You can't reason your way towards truth. But once you know the truth then, and only then, can you logically reason your way to further understanding of that truth.

Let me tell you about my great grandmother. My great grandmother had a neighbor. Her neighbor loved grandma's coffee because grandma bought premium coffee for her family.

Grandma's neighbor would borrow coffee from grandma but she was not known for her honesty.

One day grandma realized who was responsible for this uncomfortable relationship with her neighbor and she set about to rectify it. Out she went to the store and purchased a can of premium coffee just for her neighbor, but she didn't give it to her---not all at once. Instead she put it on her own pantry shelf and used this can to lend coffee to her neighbor when she came to borrow coffee.

When on occasion the neighbor lady did repay my grandmother, grandma was sure to put that coffee back into the can she had purchased for her neighbor.

Days passed. The neighbor lady asked grandma if she'd switched brands of coffee. Her coffee didn't seem to taste as good as it used to.

"No," grandma assured her, "I'm still using the same brand."

Now of course the inevitable occurred just as grandmother had known it would. The neighbor's coffee can turned up empty. When the neighbor lady came to borrow coffee on that day, grandma brought out the empty can and explained to her what had taken place.

And that was the end of the neighbor borrowing coffee.

This simple story about my great grandmother explains how to think and behave like an honest banker better than any I have ever encountered.

First of all, you have to separate your money from the money that is being inflated by the dishonest practices of bankers, politicians, and the social engineers of today. You **MUST** protect yourself against inflation! You **MUST** realize who your real opponents are and protect yourself from them!

Secondly, you have to continue to function in a world with the "legal tender" of your time. You can't just start your own currency. You'll end up in jail. You are in this world but not necessarily a part of it. As Bill Bonner so profoundly remarks, "(you) must accept that we live in a government mandated economy and get on with it – do what we can to protect what we've earned and work out ways to grow our savings over the long term...taxes, although a knotty issue, are more controllable than investment returns"[13] and therefore you need to focus on what you can control and not on what you can't. This is the power behind how Warren Buffet created his wealth, he "became the world's most successful investor by understanding how putting off tax payments can build wealth."[14] Analyze the chart below and see how investing at 6% with and without taxes affects the outcome of your profits. In a combined income tax bracket of 33%, on a $50,000 investment, there is a 50% advantage over the course of the first 12 months by not having your growth taxed! After 5 years your advantage by investing in a deferred product has climbed to over 56%. And by year 20 your advantage has reached a staggering 85.3%. Notice also, during the five year period between years 15 and 20, there is a 10.94% difference in your advantage between the deferred account and the account that is taxed. Yet this advantage between years of 1 and 5 is only 6.11%. That is why Albert Einstein called compound interest the eighth wonder of the world. As an honest banker you can control this money. By learning to control this "invisible" money (invisible because most people never see it or even know it exists,) you can become quite wealthy.

Initial Deposit $50,000	Yr	Gain -33% Taxes	Gain Without Taxes	Tax Deferring Advantage	% Tax Deferring Advantage
6% APR	1	$2,000	$3,000	$1,000	50.00%
6% APR	5	$10,833	$16,911	$6,079	56.11%
6% APR	10	$24,012	$39,542	$15,530	64.68%
6% APR	15	$40,047	$69,828	$29,781	74.36%
6% APR	20	$59,556	$110,357	$50,801	85.30%

[13] Chris Hunt's blog
[14] *Learning to Think Like Warren Buffett,* Business Week, February 14, 2005 pg. 29

Thirdly, you have to protect your family from the entitlement activists who think that what they own is theirs and what you own and produce is theirs too. You have an obligation to protect and provide for your own. In doing so, you will provide for many others besides because you can't have what you need and want in life without helping others attain what they need and want as well. However if you don't provide for your own nobody else will either.

Once you appreciate these three fundamental facts regarding wealth you're primed to comprehend how participating whole life insurance has a very long history of providing all three of these fundamental strengths for you.[15]

But just owning a "separate coffee can" (a participating whole life policy) isn't going to make your "coffee beans" grow. The growth part is up to you. All the "separate can of coffee" will provide you is a safe and secure place where your "beans" can reside... a place without inherent losses which become paramount in any other system of wealth creation.

So now consider how some of the following "bean" growers used their "coffee cans" (participating whole life insurance policies) to protect and increase their wealth. One caution.... the logic and actions demonstrated in these living examples is not generally understood by those who are still thinking and behaving like everybody else, i.e., rate of returns, annual percentage rates, and principal and interest loans. To understand what follows you **MUST** think and behave like an honest banker. And as that is the purpose of this book, please proceed to the next chapters.

---

[15] Forbes.com <u>A Financial Bunker in Scary Times</u>, J. G. 2-10-09

Real Life vs. Theory

Chapter Seven

Truth is more of a stranger than fiction. - Mark Twain

Life if full of payments: You either pay others or you pay yourself. There isn't any other option unless you are a thief or the beneficiary of charity. If you use other people's money you must pay them for the use of their money. If you use your own money then you'll lose the profit you could have earned on your money if it had been invested somewhere else... unless you pay yourself for the use of your own money.

Let me share my own story. Realizing the true cost of using my own money, I decided I should pay myself for the use of my own money. Having come to appreciate the fact that participating whole life insurance was the safest and most secure place to save my money I placed $30,000 in a policy with a small mid-western mutual life insurance company.

Why a small company? Why not a large, well known company? Why not a company with higher and/or "better" rating? Quite frankly, my decision was based chiefly on the dividend paying track record of this company which was over 100 consecutive years at that time! Besides this great dividend paying track record, this little company was still proud of their solid fiscal principles grounded on permanent whole life insurance... providing lifetime security to their policy holders! I also realized that ratings were very subjective. There are only four companies

43

responsible for the ratings of insurance companies.[16] They have been politically "blessed" with the concession to rate the insurance industry, I didn't... and still don't... place a lot of credence on these ratings. Moreover, companies highly rated by these same agencies had gone south shortly after receiving their high rating. So I based my choice of a company on their dividend track record and the dedication to their policy owners versus stock holders.

Now when I deposited my $30,000 into my participating whole life insurance policy the insurance company contractually guaranteed me the right to borrow up to $22,000 immediately. So I did.

Borrowing that $22,000 I purchased goods and services which I normally would have purchased using my income. In doing so I created cash flow. Now the $22,000 I would have spent of my income on goods and services was free to use elsewhere.

Desiring to behave like an honest banker I used this cash flow to begin paying off the loan to the insurance company, understanding that this was the way an honest banker makes money, by charging interest to borrowers. I knew, therefore, that I'd need to pay the insurance company's loan back over time so the interest would accrue and benefit me because I owned a participating policy with that company. Paying it all back immediately would not have

---

[16] **A.M. Best Company** (www.ambest.com) is the leading provider of ratings for the insurance industry. **The Fitch Ratings Insurance Group** (www.fitchibca.com) provides ratings and research on insurance companies worldwide. **Moody's** www.moodys.com) provides financial strength ratings for life insurance companies. **Standard & Poor's** (www.sandp.com) provides ratings and research on insurance companies.

accrued any interest. Thus I planned on taking 5 years to pay this loan back.

Having recognized that honest bankers charge more than what they pay their depositors I realized that this extra interest was the honest banker's profit (wage earned,) not usury or some other gross evil which many have classified it. And so accordingly I made sure to be honest with myself. Fact is I doubled the interest rate which the company was asking on the loan! The insurance company was charging 6% but I paid the loan back at 12%. This was twice the velocity of what the insurance company requested. And this, they were charging because they knew they needed that much in order to make my policy perform according to the contractual illustration they had provided me. But I knew that any extra interest I paid would increase the face value of my policy because it would purchase more death benefit. Furthermore, I understood that by increasing the face value I was guaranteed to see an increase in the cash value... money that I could borrow from the insurance company. It was a win-win. The company had 100% of what they needed and I had 100% of what I desired. For the first time in my life I had the volume of interest working for me instead of the bankers, politicians and social engineers of the world!

Over the life of that first loan I paid the insurance company back $29,362.67. This is $3,843.37 more than what the insurance company requested ($25,519.30.) But it was only $64.06 more per month ($489.38 vs. $425.32.) Besides, I knew where it was all going to end up. So the extra $64.06 monthly payment wasn't an issue with me. Instead I eagerly and easily paid it by utilizing the extra cash flow which the policy loan had produced in the first place. The bottom line was this: Paying extra interest didn't lower my standard of living...it actually increased it!

Each proceeding year, over the next four years, I paid myself first by depositing $30,000.00 of premium payments from my income into this same participating whole life insurance policy. While every six months or so I continued to borrow from the life insurance company the maximum amount that I was permitted to borrow in accordance to my contract... which was an ever increasing amount of cash value.

At the end of the first six months I had repaid $2,936.27 on the first $22,000.00 insurance policy loan. Appreciating the fact that this $2,936.27 was money that was just going to sit around I borrowed it out and put it to work purchasing other goods and services...all of which I'd normally have used my income to purchase. This again produced $2,936.27 of extra cash flow by freeing up the same amount of income which would have been used on the same purchases had I not borrowed from my policy's cash values to spend instead. This increased cash flow allowed me to pay back the new loan at $138.22 per month over the next two years...an additional $381.02 ($3,317.29 - $2,936.27 = $381.02.) Now I had the velocity of money working in my favor without me having to work any harder or any longer...my money working for me...what a simple but profound process!

At this point some people begin to feel overwhelmed by the number of loans that could be processed in this manner and how they are ever going to keep track of them all. That is why we have developed a software program to keep track of this for us we make that software available for you. Remember, this is how honest bankers earn their profit and honest bankers have software to keep track of their banking and you need to have a software program too. It isn't hard even though there is going to be a learning curve for you.

46

But that is why you need an experienced coach to help you along...one who has already mastered this process and is personally practicing the self-financing game. The profits earned will be well worth your time spent during the learning curve.

You see, when I learned to appreciate the fact that the only reason anybody purchases anything on time is that they can afford the monthly payments, it wasn't difficult for me to structure the payments back to myself accordingly, (i.e., payments that I could afford.) I was beginning to think and behave like an honest banker making financial arrangements so that my money would stretch over time while affording me the luxury of designing my own affordable payments. Each time I did this more cash flow was liberated because my income wasn't needed to purchase goods and services when the money being borrowed from the insurance company was purchasing those goods and services.

Over time our standard of living increased without me having to work any longer or harder because now we were (and still are) earning the wages of an honest banker--- interest. You see all the extra interest I pay on my policy loans, really goes towards additional premium payments, increasing my death benefit, which in turn increases my cash values. When the day is done, the interest which I've paid to the company on these policy loans has returned to me in the form of extra premiums paid through dividends earned. Therefore who have I really been paying all that extra interest to?

This process is contrary to what everybody else in the financial world will tell you. You see, everybody else will tell you to keep your principal safe, locked up, on deposit or invested in someone else's bank. Then, eventually it will produce enough interest on which you can live. But, when you think and behave like an honest banker you'll want to put your principal to work and by doing so you'll be able to afford to pay yourself the interest you now pay to others (or simply lose when you pay cash.) **The interest you pay yourself will significantly increase your policy face value which in turn will produce even more principal (cash value) for you to borrow and use, thus creating a new and improved lifestyle for you and your loved ones. All it takes is honesty...honesty in paying yourself first (paying premiums) and honesty in paying yourself back (paying back the insurance company on the loans they gave you with interest.)**

I've now been self-financing like this for over 5 years. I've continued to borrow from this original policy and I've continued to pay the loans back with a greater amount of interest than what the insurance company has requested. My face value in this original policy has exceeded the projected illustrated value of the insurance company by nearly $100,000 to date. This increased face value has also increased the total amount of money the insurance company will lend to me. And I rest soundly every night assured that if something should happen to me and I should meet my Creator, I have no debt! That's because the insurance company will pay off my loans upon my death and give the balance of my death benefit to my loved ones.

Over these past 5 plus years, the interest that I've paid to the insurance company has exceeded what this one policy will hold (that is because I have paid more interest than what the company requested.) That hasn't created a problem but has simply led me to create a larger "coffee can" so that I can control those profits and maintain liquidity. This means that I have used all that extra interest to purchase more participating whole life policies. These policies have been purchased on my life, my wife's life, my children's lives and the lives of other insurable interests which I have...business partners, siblings, employees, etc. Have you ever heard of a bank having too many depositors? Well, once you understand that there is absolutely no better place to put your money, and still maintain liquidity than participating whole life insurance, you'll be wanting to place more of these policies under your ownership because each one of them behaves just like another depositor in your self-financing system.

And so I've come to know in Real Life... firsthand... what my mentor told me years ago...! **"Always bank with it first!"** Which candidly means this: Pay your premiums before you spend your money anywhere else. In doing so, you will always have the use of the money which the insurance company contractually guarantees to loan to you on request, but at the same time your money (from your income) will be freed-up to pay back those loans with extra interest... therefore increasing the amount of money you can borrow next time. Oh, and by the way, you'll still be earning a guaranteed profit... the guaranteed cash value increases plus any declared dividends which the insurance company has contracted to pay you on your policy.

———

This sounds like good stuff huh? Well that's because it is! When you contact our office at Life Benefits, Inc. you will get the best of the best... best service, best coaching, best team, because we believe you deserve our best. Besides, why would you want anything less?

Call our office 1-866-502-2777 or email us:
team@life-benefits.com

What Are Others Doing?

Chapter Eight

Truth persuades by teaching, but does not teach by persuading. - *Quintus Septimius Tertullianus*

Now let's hear from some others who've honestly applied the concepts contained in this book to their own life. Each of these individuals is well known to me. Other than their name (I've used different names to protect privacy) they would tell you their story just as I have reported it here. Our clients are not ashamed or bashful of letting others know what thinking and behaving like an honest banker has done for their lives.

You see, I want to be there helping to coach and learning from the people who've been touched by these life changing concepts. The world needs more honest bankers! So check our website (www.life-benefits.com) regularly to see where and when our next event will be held. Perhaps it will be in a location near you or a place that you would like to travel and visit. Your Wealth Team here at Life Benefits, Inc. looks forward to meeting and working with you.

————

Amy
Amy was beside herself. Having been a productive business owner for many years she was caught between a rock and a hard place. Not yet old enough to draw upon her annuities, which had been funded by the sale of her business, but too old (she thought) to start a new venture in life. Amy was hardly able to live on what social security

was paying her. With a home that was nearly paid for she had no deductions and little income. Amy was scared! With no family or loved ones to fall back on she spent her time being frugal and penny wise.

But once Amy understood how to think and behave like an honest banker she knew what to do.

Amy processed a reverse mortgage on her home. With the proceeds of this reverse mortgage Amy was able to fund two life insurance policies that were designed for her special needs. The loans from these polices have allowed Amy to travel abroad as well as in the states. But more importantly than her travels, Amy has been able to spend more of her time helping others who are less fortunate than herself because she doesn't have to spend so much time fretting and pinching pennies.

Oh, and when Amy does graduate from this life, her two policies will have enough death benefit that her reverse mortgage can be redeemed, if that is what is desired.

Bill and Kathy
Consider Bill and Kathy. Early sixties, not high income, care provider of a parent that was in his later stages of life.

But grasping the truth behind **"Why You Should and Can Be Rich"** they took their life investments (their qualified plans,) cashed them in and purchased participating whole life insurance policies on both of their lives.

Using their meager earnings this couple diligently borrowed the cash values from their policies and paid those loans back by creating an affordable payment and time frame suited just for them.

This couple didn't consume the increased cash flow which this process inherently frees up and so within a couple years they began to notice the increased life style they were afforded by this process. This was a level of comfort which wasn't permissible prior to their learning how to think and behave like an honest banker with their own money.

Then it happened. The aging parent passed away leaving a large sum of money. Because Bill and Kathy had already learned the process of thinking and behaving like honest bankers they were able to retain thousands of dollars from this inheritance by placing it into the life insurance policies they already owned...and they were able to purchase even more on their lives to secure their retirement and to bless the next generation.

Without those first couple of years and their willingness to understand WHY they should be rich, this wonderful couple would have forfeited thousands of dollars in service fees to the financial planner who wanted to "help" them plan for their future. Now they have extra cash flow and a legacy to leave for their children and the charity works that they have spent their lifetime supporting.

Mike
Watching his variable life insurance (VUL) product lose value daily, Mike was desperate. The major insurance company that he had purchased his variable life insurance policy from nearly 15 years earlier was not willing to work with him in transferring his policy cash values into a participating whole life insurance policy. Mike understood he had to act fast in order to protect what cash values were left in his VUL policy before it was all gone! Mike understood WHY he should be rich but he was learning the

best way to accomplish this… and it wasn't by trusting the market or his financial planners but rather it was by thinking and acting like an honest banker with his own money.

So Mike paid a "small" fee to transfer the non-performing VUL policy to another smaller mutual company that was willing to offer him a participating whole life insurance policy.

Since then Mike has borrowed his money from the new policy, which he rescued from that VUL policy, and has used it to pay off his office building and finance several pieces of equipment for his business.

Now Mike is paying the insurance company back like an honest banker, knowing that those funds will go to purchase more face value in his new participating policy. But the principal on those loans will continue to be used to finance his needs and expenses for years to come adding wealth that he now controls--- not the insurance company or Wall Street or anybody else for that matter.

Mike is now profiting on what he had been losing when he owned that VUL policy, but it's even better than that because now the growth he is experiencing will never face income taxes as long as he continues to think and behave like an honest banker.

Lisa
Strapped and desperate for cash flow, Lisa was seriously contemplating bankruptcy. But when the rubber met the road she just couldn't do it. She knew deep down that she couldn't walk away from those debts that she herself had created.

After we explained how honest bankers make money, Lisa was ready to go. She purchased three policies, one on herself and one on each of her two children.

Following the advice given; borrowing money from the insurance company and paying the insurance company back the interest on the loans taken, Lisa paid off over $40,000.00 of debt in the first 12 months. By month 18 she had paid off nearly all her creditors and with the refinancing of a home purchased on a credit card, she is now learning what financial freedom really is! And it's not working harder and longer to pay off debts.

You see, Lisa has done all this without having to take a second job, work longer hours or even sell off her personal possessions. She hasn't even had to take a loss on her debts to accomplish this. Yet she was told the only way out was bankruptcy!

Needless to say, Lisa tells everybody about her journey. But interestingly enough, very few believe her story. They just can't figure it out. That's why everybody needs a coach.

Edward and Rose
Too old to purchase a policy on their own lives to make it worth their time and effort, Edward and Rose turned to their children.

Purchasing participating whole life insurance policies on their children, this couple who are now in their 80's, used the money (the flow of money makes money) from these policies just like an honest banker would do.

When the cash flow increase became unmistakably apparent to them they simply loaned trusted family members the "extra" money which increased their standard of living significantly.

Who says you're too old?

Carl

Wanting to start his newly born grandson on the journey to becoming rich early, Carl purchased a small policy on his grandson Trevor.

Carl will pay an average of $2.74 a day for the first 20 years of Trevor's life which will provide Trevor with over $307,000 of cash value when he turns 70. For a $20,002.00 dollar investment in his grandson's life Carl has provided Trevor with a $286,998 return.

Now, if grandpa Carl is able to teach his grandson how to think and behave like an honest banker, then Trevor will be able to recover all the money he spends for cars, education, vacations, etc., and all that money will be there for him besides the $286,998 when he reaches his golden years.

Do you know anybody too young to start?

Each of the real life stories[17] above are clients of mine. Every one of them started exactly where you are...not knowing WHY you should and can be rich and not being able to think and behave like an honest banker. And so did yours truly.

---

[17] Names have been changed to protect privacy.

You see, everybody has to start somewhere. But the very best place to start is where you're at right now! Nobody who is currently practicing the art of being rich has ever told me that they wished they had waited a few more years before they'd started. On the other hand many...most have said that they wished they'd known about this sooner so they could have conducted their lives accordingly.

Thinking and behaving like an honest banker begins right where you're at. You're never too old, too young, too poor or too rich. You can be too ignorant, and you could have even been a bit too foolish in the past. But with passion, self- discipline and proper coaching you can learn to think and behave like an honest banker with your own money and become extremely wealthy. You **can** secure the profits that are designed for you to enjoy. And you can still leave greater wealth and benefits to your loved ones and charitable causes by acting now!

Call our office 1-866-502-2777 or email us: team@life-benefits.com we're here for you.

"You Are Here"

Chapter Nine

The Best Place to Start

Last summer our family headed off to one of our favorite parks...Silver Falls State Park. There's an 8.5 mile hiking trail with 10 waterfalls along the way. The South Falls is the most frequently visited of the falls; ample parking, lots of picnicking places and the largest, most spectacular waterfall. At the head of the trail we stopped at the kiosk and found our spot **"You Are Here."** We planned to walk to South Falls and instead of taking the loop back we were hoping to walk on to the Lower South Falls as well. You see, we had some 3 year old legs along with us, so we had to accommodate. Good news is: We made it, and we made it back! Sure, it took some help from some strong armed older brothers, but we made it! Someday we hope to make it further along the trail to see falls we haven't seen in many years...Drake Falls, Twin Falls and Double Falls. But we're not there yet. We have limitations right now.

Recently we were on vacation and went to a large shopping mall. We parked and entered the mall at Borders. We made our way into the interior mall and found the kiosk, again looking for the words **"You Are Here."** We found where we were and then looked at where we wanted to go. That day it was Nordstrom. We needed to cross to the other side of the mall and walk almost to the other end to get there. And this set me to thinking...

Every day we have people calling our office with their financial dreams...where they'd like to be. They want to pay off their house, retire in five years, buy a new car, save on taxes, build retirement income, fund college tuition etc.

Those dreams are what motivate people to move forward. Good. But first we have to find the spot that says **"You Are Here."** That's where you've got to start, *but* that's not what most people want to hear. Then comes the groan that I recognize so well, "I wish I had known about this process years ago," or "I wish I had started this sooner." And yet from there sometimes they actually decide it would be better if they leave the mall!...even give up their parking space and try to enter from some other door...closer to their desired destination.

Now here's where my little analogy breaks down because they could do that, couldn't they? But even with the real mall, that's not too practical, is it? They probably won't save any time in getting to Nordstrom. Our mall experience tells us that the best way to get there is to start walking. It's the same in the realm of finances, but many people leave "the mall", thinking they'll go get out of debt first, win the lottery or somehow get more financially fit before beginning the journey. They think that when they have more money they'll be ready to take steps to greater financial freedom. But that's like saying you'll start exercising when you become more physically fit. It doesn't work that way, does it? (Too bad, I might add!) That's "teenage" thinking...without proper reasoning. You don't give your car keys to your 16 year old son to show you how responsible he can be. No, you give him the car keys when he's proved his responsibility.

Mainstream financing methods have most people treading water...not really going anywhere, and yes, drowning too! Debt and aggressive taxation are keeping people in slavery. But when you play the game by the rule found in this book you own the vehicle and the tools to get you to where you want to go...faster. So, when is it time to start thinking and behaving like an honest banker? Today, right now, right where you are! With debt? You'll be able to eliminate it faster. Need a new car" You'll be money ahead. Need to pay off your mortgage, fund tuition, "retire"? Let's find the sign that says **"You Are Here,"** then we can see the path to where you want to go. Zig Ziglar says, "You don't have to be great to start, but you have to start to be great!" One of the coaches here at Life Benefits, Inc. can help you get started right where you are with your current finances, so that *you'll be fit and able to go where you want to go!* How much money does it take? That depends on where you are and where you desire to go!

Let's look at your financial kiosk so we can find the **"You Are Here."** Then we can look at the best path for you to start the journey to your dreams. Start with the end in mind, but realize it's a journey. To begin with you may not be able to finance your whole mortgage, your entire business overhead or your child's tuition. But you may be able to finance your car, some business equipment, or textbooks. And by financing these things you'll be closer to your dream of financing those bigger items. And yes, we know you want to finance your retirement too, perhaps financing your next vacation will be just the thing to help you do that! Incredible thought, isn't it?

I know it'll be a few more years before I see Drake Falls, Twin Falls and Double Falls again, but in the meantime there's no sense in missing out on South Falls...it's breathtaking. And so is the journey of learning to think and behave like an honest banker. Contact us at 866-502-2777 and we can coach you along the way...but start now!

———

Remember successful people start somewhere. It doesn't matter where, as long as you start, and the start that you make will be enough to lead you to greater success.

Stories from Clients

Chapter Ten

"Your time is limited, so don't waste it ... Don't be trapped by dogma – which is living with the results of other people's thinking." – Steve Jobs

Now you get to hear from some of our clients as they share their stories with you. Enjoy!

———

This process has been positive for me in multiple ways. One, it has given me more security for my family in case of my untimely death, two, it has given me the ability and accountability to invest money and do so safely in today's market, and thirdly it has given me the ability to have invested money available for use at my discretion and in my timing.

Here is one example. Last year my son was nearing 16 and we needed to provide a car for him for his school commute. We knew of a neighbor that had a perfect car for him that was for sale. Because we had the money available in our own privatized banking system, we were able to take advantage of buying the car within a couple of days. We saved big time buying from a private owner as the price was much lower than we could have found otherwise, we did not have to pay sales tax to a private buyer, and we avoided paying any interest to a bank, whose rate would have been much higher than buying from a private seller! Along with that we have been able to set up our own payment plan with interest and pay ourselves back in a year. Now the money is available again for whatever we choose to use it for rather than in a banker's pocket waiting for me to borrow from them again!

This is a great process... it allows you to gain more benefits than the standard market system which our country has become so ingrained in today. -Dr. O.

———

I would like to share our story.

Four years ago, my wife, Nena told me about becoming a banker by purchasing whole life insurance. This was a banking concept which Tom McFie was introducing to her. My mind was not open to any banking or insurance program. Nena had money in one of her pension plans and decided to use those funds to purchase a policy.

As happens every year property taxes came due. We were discussing how we were going to pay the taxes. I usually take funds from our checking or saving accounts and at times get a loan from a local bank. Nena asked me to let her pay the taxes through her insurance policy. She said all I had to do was make payments back into an account she had opened for this banking purpose. Of course, I was open to see how this would work out! She received the money from the insurance company and paid the property taxes. I made a few payments to "her" insurance policy. A few months later, income taxes were due. Again we used the insurance policy funds to pay our taxes. I became more interested in this concept.

I started to accompany Nena to the monthly "bankers" meetings with Tom McFie. I started to see and understand the concept of the banking equation. Meeting and hearing the stories shared by the others also were of great assistance.

It was not until two years ago, that I accompanied Nena to a meeting about "The Problem" with Americans' spending habits. The explanation of how we finance everything we purchase... and how the banks make money on the interest they earn on "our" money was explained by using the airplane phenomenon. I thought, "This makes sense."

One year ago, I purchased my own whole life insurance policy. I immediately put the money to work. Whenever I needed additional money I would make big payments to our policies and then ask for a loan. But, the reality was that I was not following the concept to the full extent. I was not making payments directly into our banking account. I was skipping this very important step. It was not until a few weeks ago that I woke up at 3am and realized that in order to make the process work correctly, I needed to make monthly payments on each and every loan I had taken from our policies.

I no longer have doubts. I have questions. I will always have questions.

Tom, Michele and family, thank you so much for introducing and sharing this very important life changing concept to us.

God bless you, Raul

————

This process has given us hope for our finances. We can now see that it is possible to get out of debt! And to actually have the possibility of retirement income. After building a new house that ended up costing way more than anticipated, combined with a tough economy (my husband and I both work in retail), our financial future looked pretty dismal. We discussed selling the house, but with the real estate market the way it is, that was unlikely to happen. Thanks to Tom's enlightening me we now have a plan that will allow us to be out of debt within 7 to 10 years by making the same monthly payments we were making already, AND to have accumulated a large cash value in a life policy in the process. Thank you, Tom! –Tammy

———

This past summer our daughter was visiting us. She was driving a 1970's Volkswagen camper van with over 500,000 miles on it. She loved it and had driven it for over 10 years. Her mother and I did not think it was a safe vehicle to drive and were happy when a call came from Erin three weeks later that the van had imploded in the mountains of Idaho. Four days later, she had decided on a new SUV and insisted on pulling $15,000 from her savings along with a loan for the remainder of the unit. I advised her to keep her money in savings and we would borrow the entire amount from our life insurance policy. Erin was totally against that as she hates being any deeper in debt than is necessary. After a lot of explaining how the life insurance process works from us and Tom, she finally started to understand the benefit of borrowing from our policy. Her eyes were opened further when it took just three minutes to arrange the policy loan. It is a remarkably easy process. Three days later Erin was very happy driving back to school in her new SUV and we were extremely happy to have her in a safe vehicle, plus we were able to use some of our policy cash value.

What a wonderful feeling of freedom the infinite banking system is and a great way to do business!

We have been using the banking concept for two years now and are very grateful.

Roger & Jan

———

As an émigré to this country I have worked hard to make things nicer for my family than where I grew up. When Tom approached me with this concept I realized this was an opportunity to provide something more for my family.

I began with what I could afford purchasing a policy on my own life. I borrowed from this policy to purchase more equipment for my business, paying myself (policy) back in time as I could afford to. My business is seasonal and the flexibility that I have over how frequently the payments go back to the policy are very beneficial for me. I can make larger payments when the work is coming in and no payments when I am seasonally without an income.

Well, to make a long story short I've paid property taxes, and purchased small pieces of equipment and have paid myself back on each of those policy loans. And each time I do there is more cash value to borrow.

This year was very exciting. My son who is entering into a business related to my own needed to purchase a large piece of equipment which requires a special license to own and operate. I've been unable to secure that license yet, but my son has and I was able to loan him the money necessary to purchase the equipment on his license. He will be able to operate this equipment and hire others to do so as well. That means he won't have to work as hard as I have in order to support and raise his family.

Furthermore, as he pays the loan back to me, I'm going to put the repayments back into my policy which will just make my death benefit get bigger. And of course my son will benefit from that someday too. - A Father

---

Two years ago, a very wise man explained this concept to us. He suggested that one way to make this concept work very efficiently for us was to put my whole income into participating whole life insurance premiums and draw money for living expenses. I did just that. It has been very profitable for us. Now the two ways to accumulate money is to have money working or man working. When I retired, I improved on this principle. We now have money working for us through because of our participating whole life insurance policies, but as my wife is still working, I now have woman working instead of me (man) working. I am very happy with the entire situation! – Roger

---

Our story is that we are still in the first year.

What I can say so far: I enjoy this hands-on management of our money. I enjoy all the fringe benefits that life insurance provides. Margin makes more margin. Confidence breeds more confidence. –Ben

---

Well, we have been able to give our home considerable upgrades that were necessary and uplifting; pay off all credit card debt; create some residual income; provide backup investment loans to our corporation; give to charity more substantially; provide some medical needs not covered under a health plan; pay for unexpected needs and still have more to continue for future growth – all of which were impossible three years ago. (This happened this week:) Don'tcha just love it when a banker calls up and asks me "what are you going to do with all that money???" – translation: "You have a lot of money and *WE* want to make money with it, please; we'll give you a good deal .025% interest." Not joking. He actually offered that. Unreal. When I can make at least 10% why in the world would I loan it to the bank at .025% or "double the deal with a 11-month CD at 2%" -- why in the world would I take him up on that??!! This is the second time the bank has called me asking me that. I love it. Tables are topsy-turvy for the first time in my life. – R. H.

Just wanted to give you an update on my journey... I have all debts paid except student loans and my mortgage and all loan repayments are set up. I have the corporate loan done and also set up. Right now I have around $8000 per month being paid into my separate account and it feels great to pay myself instead of the banks!

I talked to the agent who has my boys' whole life policies- that was quite a treat! I had him switch them to yearly premiums. He basically told me I was an idiot to borrow money from the accounts to pay any debt. He also said it's not fair to the rest of the policy holders for me to take my money out!! Funny thing is, 2 days later, he calls me back and asked where I heard about the plan I was using. He apparently had a group call him asking about it and wanted me to tell him how it works! I said, "You obviously know a lot more than I do, you figure it out". – Dr. F.

We always thought we were on the right track regarding our finances. When we were first introduced to the banking concept we were a little skeptical and hesitant, but the more we learned about it the more excited we became about the potential that Banking offered. After our first loan we felt that we were on a good track and more comfortable and at ease with the idea despite how unconventional the banking concept was. After the second loan in our second year we noticed a tremendous freedom that came from this new banking method. We now had a better cash flow and were able to meet our financial needs easier and with less stress than ever before. We have started our second policy now that we are about to start our third year. We are so excited about the future of our finances and are truly blessed by the opportunities that we have had to support and bless others financially. This has allowed our charitable giving to increase without any detriment to our financial well-being. The freedom and security that provided has exceeded our expectations and has been a true blessing. I encourage anyone to jump in head first. - S and T

———

Our family is thankful for your family and all of your patience in instructing and educating us in this concept. It has been a blessing to have been afforded the ability to purchase our clinic building, digital x-ray, other equipment, and pay bills with trough this system of self-fianancing. I had heard many so called "financial experts" talk about financial freedom, but it tends to be financial freedom at some future, often unspecified, date. We are not financially independent yet, but we did have far greater financial freedom in 2010 as result of your work with us. We also have a plan for even greater financial freedom each year in the future. Perhaps the thing we look forward to the most is the freedom to tithe more freely each year. We also look forward to creative things we can do with our money. These would be things that we are passionate about rather than investing in the market with all of its risks and with companies we have no allegiance to whatsoever. We love knowing that our children will know the Austrian monetary system and will have participating whole life insurance policies of their own one day. This knowledge will save them, and their children, from the reliance of borrowing from others and losing their financial freedom by doing so. Your family has much to be proud of. We are happy to have you as our mentors and friends. –Dr. B. and Family

———

Ever since I had graduated from college and started my working career I have been skeptical of anything related to investing and financing; especially things such as stocks and bonds, retirement funds etc. All those methods would take the money out of my control and lock it away where it was difficult to access, if at all, and was subject to the whims of the market. This system was the first financial method that ever made any sense. Here I am able to grow my funds and use them at the same time!

This is something I truly believe in and encourage my friends and anyone who will listen to check this out for themselves. –Nathan

———

When I came across this concept, I had been a chiropractor for about 10 years. The learning that I've had about how to run a business and make it profitable has all come by reading books of various sorts. From this reading I would apply the fore mentioned advice in real business life and see the results. In this way I was able to figure out what works and what doesn't. But I kept running into the same problem... not enough cash backup and not enough credit. When I met Tom I was carrying a lot of credit card debt and was paying a lot of money to use someone else's money. This system is the only system that has allowed me to keep my money working for me. I also discovered that it is a very practical way of creating a cash savings fund that is liquid and safe. A big turning point for me was the beginning of the third year of owning the policy. That was the final turn on the mental screw of belief in the system working for me. –Dr. D

___

Thanks for taking the time to teach me the process. I almost got to reap some additional early death benefits and though I know my family would have been devastated God would have used it to His glory and I would have left enough to meet (my wife's) needs. Not exactly my children's, children, but now I have more time. –Kurt

___

Thank You! It is exactly the way it is! -Iza

___

We know your time is valuable and we want to respect it. For your convenience, here is the necessary information you will need, to contact one of us at Life Benefits, Inc. by phone or email. We look forward to talking with you!

Phone: **1-866-502-2777**   Email: <u>team@life-benefits.com</u>

"Thank you so much for taking the time to explain...it really helped..."

---Stephanie, Florida

Now we just need to decide what to spend the money on."

---Byron, Oregon

"Have I told you how much I appreciate your patience in educating us?"   --- Dr. Jay, Minnesota

"I strongly recommend this to anyone looking for a proven method to take them to financial freedom."

---Dr. Erich Breitenmoser, California

"Dr. McFie is very knowledgeable."

---Dr. Mareechi Duvvuri, Oregon

"I have been associated both professionally and personally with Dr. McFie...I do highly trust this fine man and I have no qualms in telling you that you can do the same."

---Dr. Todd Osborne, Georgia

"Again thank you Tom and Michele for sharing this."

---Dr. Chris Robinson, Oregon.

"WOW!! This makes sense!!"

---Smile, Anonymous

"Tom and Michele have been a huge help in our success."

---Jackie, Oregon

"We are so excited to be paying ourselves the interest we have been paying to creditors all these years!"

---Janice, Oregon

"This is the most powerful concept in finance today ignore it at your own peril."   ---Matthew, Colorado

"...my life will be better financially...God Bless you."
---Nena, Oregon

"You are a blessing to us and we don't take that lightly."
---Walt and Ruth Ann, Oregon

"...thank you for your quick response!!! You scored big points!"
---Scott, Washington

"Thanks for all you've done for us...!"
---George, Virginia

"(My friend) spent hours with me trying to explain this concept... I wish he would've just had me read the book."
---Phil, Oregon

Glossary

Annual Percentage Rate: the interest rate for a whole year (annualized), rather than just a monthly fee/rate.

Annual Rate of Return: also known as **return on investment (ROI)**, **rate of profit** or sometimes just **return**, the ratio of money gained or lost (whether realized or unrealized) on an investment.

Banking Equation: the flow of money from one entity to another facilitated by an intermediate who earns a profit from the transaction.

Borrow: to receive (something) from somebody temporarily.

Capital: the factor of production, used to create goods or services, that is not itself significantly consumed (though it may depreciate) in the production process.

Cash Value: also called the cash surrender value or surrender value, the cash amount offered to the policy owner by the issuing life carrier upon cancellation of the contract.

Charity: the giving to worthy causes or people in need.

Death Benefit: the amount on a life insurance policy or pension that is payable to the beneficiary when the insured passes away. Also known as a "survivor benefit".

Debt: that which is owed.

Depositors: to give over or entrust for safekeeping, to put (money) in a bank or financial account, to give as partial payment or security.

Deposits: something (usually money) given.

Dividends: A distribution of a portion of a company's earnings, decided by the board of directors, in participating whole life insurance classified as a return of premium and therefore not taxable.

Equity: the value of an ownership interest in property.

Face Value: the nominal value or dollar value of a policy as stated by the issuer.

Federal Reserve: The Federal Reserve System is the central banking system of the United States. It was created in 1913 with the enactment of the Federal Reserve Act.

Fraudulent: a fraud is an intentional deception made for personal gain or to damage another individual; the related adjective is fraudulent.

Freedom: the absence of interference with the sovereignty of an individual by the use of coercion or aggression.

Economic freedom: the freedom to produce, trade and consume any goods and services acquired without the use of force, fraud or theft.

G.A.M.E. guaranteed, available, manageable, equity.

Government: the particular group of people, the administrative bureaucracy, who control a state at a given time.

Imagination: the work of the mind that helps create.

Inflation: an erosion in the purchasing power of money – a loss of real value in the internal medium of exchange and unit of account in the economy.

Interest: a fee paid on borrowed assets, the price paid for the use of borrowed money, or money earned on deposited funds.

Interest Only Loan: a loan in which, for a set term, the borrower pays only the interest on the principal balance, with the principal balance unchanged.

Investment: the commitment of money or capital to the purchase of financial instruments or other assets in the hope of earning a profitable return.

Legal Tender: a medium of payment allowed by law or recognized by a legal system to be valid for meeting financial obligations.

Participating Whole Life Insurance: known as a with-profits policy the insurance company shares the excess profits (variously called dividends or refunds in the USA) with the policyholder. Typically these refunds are not taxable because they are considered an overcharge of premium... the greater the overcharge by the company, the greater the refund/dividend. For a mutual life insurance company, participation also implies a degree of ownership of the mutuality.

Payment: the transfer of wealth from one party (such as a person or company) to another.

Poverty: the lack of basic human needs.

Premium: an amount paid or payable, often in installments.

Principal: the amount borrowed... the portion of a payment which is not interest. In a loan amortization schedule, the principal and interest are separated, indicating which part of the payment goes to paying off the principal, and which part is used to pay interest.

Privatized Banking: where the individual owns, controls and therefore profits from the functions which a conventional bank or financial institution would typically own and control (as far as lending and loaning are concerned.)

Refinance: the replacement of an existing debt obligation with a debt obligation under different terms.

Religion: a set of beliefs concerning the cause, nature, and purpose of life and the universe.

Reserves: a stockpile.

Risk: the deviation of one or more results of one or more future events from their expected value. Technically, the value of those results may be positive or negative.

Saving: income not spent, or deferred consumption.

Schooling: The concept of grouping students together in a centralized location.

Slavery: a system under which people are treated as property and are forced to work.

Taxes: a fee charged to pay for government expenditure.

Usury: originally was the interest charged on loans; this included charging a fee for the use of money, such as at a bureau de change. Today, usury commonly is the charging of unreasonable or relatively high rates of interest. The term is largely derived from Christian religious principles.

Wage: something received by workers in exchange for their labor and time.

Wealth: the abundance of valuable resources or possessions (material or spiritual,) or the control of such assets.

Wisdom: a deep understanding and realizing of people, things, events or situations, resulting in the ability to choose or act to consistently produce the optimum results with a minimum of time and energy.

YFG
Your Financial **G**.A.M.E.™ a trademarked phrase of Life Benefits Inc. and Your Wealth Team.

Yield: the amount of profit that returns to the owner.

Index

A

Annual Percentage Rate (APR) *10, 11, 13, 41*
Annual Rate of Return *8, 13*

B

Banking Equation *7, 27, 64*
<u>Becoming Your Own Banker</u> .. xii, 51
Bonner, Bill *40*
Borrow...*xi, 22, 25, 26, 28, 39, 40, 44, 45, 46, 48, 49, 64, 66, 67*
Buffet, Warren *41*

C

Capital *6, 7*
Cash Value..*21, 22, 29, 30, 45, 46, 47, 48, 52, 53, 56, 66, 67*
Charity *24, 31, 43*
Chesterton, G. K. *39*
Coffee *39, 40, 42, 48*
Compound Interest *9*

D

Death Benefit....*21, 22, 31, 45, 47, 48, 52, 68*
Debt ... *ix, x, xii, 19, 23, 24, 48, 55, 60, 61, 65, 66, 71*
Depositors..................*6, 7, 8, 9, 49*
Deposits *5, 8*

E

Einstein, Albert.......................... *41*
Equity *13*
Exchange *1, 6, 7*

F

Face Value..*21, 22, 29, 30, 31, 45, 48, 54*
Federal Reserve *2, 3*
Fraudulent................................. *8*
Freedom..*x, 15, 16, 18, 23, 24, 55, 60, 66, 70, 71*
Friedman, Milton *5*

G

Gold................................ *1, 2, 5*
Goldsmiths................................. *1*
Goudge, Elizabeth *15*
Government *13, 16, 18, 40*

I

Imagination............................... *15*
Inflation *2, 3, 4, 8, 40*
Interest..*20, 22, 25, 26, 27, 28, 29, 30, 31, 41, 42, 44, 45, 47, 48, 49, 55, 63, 65, 73*
Interest Only Loan *12, 13*
Inventories *7*
Investment *22, 34, 41, 56*
Investments............................... *34*

J

Jefferson, Thomas..................... *17*
Jobs, Steve *63*

K

Knowledge............................... *16*

L

Lapin, Rabbi Daniel.................. *33*
Legal Tender.......................... *3, 40*

Lenin, Vladimir *1*

N

Nash, R. Nelson .... *xii*, *xv*
Newton, Sir Isaac *16*

O

Orwell, George *33*

P

Participating Whole Life
  Insurance *xiv*, *21*, *29*, *30*, *31*, *42*,
  43, *44*, *46*, *49*, *52*, *53*, *54*, *55*
Payment ....*xi*, *10*, *12*, *45*, *52*, *63*
Payments *6*, *10*, *11*, *12*, *41*, *43*, *46*,
  47, *64*, *65*, *66*, *67*
Poverty *16*, *17*, *18*, *36*
Principle....*8*, *9*, *12*, *30*, *42*, *47*, *48*,
  54, *68*
Privatized Banking *63*

R

R. Nelson Nash i
Rate of Return *6*, *8*, *9*, *10*, *21*
Read, Leonard *18*
Refinance *10*, *11*
Religion *8*
Reserves *2*, *3*, *7*
Responsibility *13*, *18*, *60*
Risk *34*, *35*

S

Saving ... *23*, *25*, *28*, *29*, *40*, *64*, *66*,
  71, *72*
Schooling *13*
Shakespeare *36*
Silver *5*
Slavery *4*, *8*, *16*, *23*, *60*

T

Taxes ... *xii*, *xiv*, *19*, *40*, *41*, *54*, *59*,
  64, *67*
Tertullianus, Quintus Septimius 51
Tomlin, Lily *19*
Twain, Mark *43*

U

Usury *7*, *8*, *45*

W

Wage *7*, *26*, *37*, *45*
Wealth *i*, *3*, *15*, *16*, *17*, *23*, *25*, *33*,
  34, *36*, *37*, *41*, *42*, *54*, *57*
Wisdom *16*, *18*

Y

Yield *9*, *19*, *21*

References

The Bible

The Bill of Rights to the Constitution of these United States of America

The Constitution of these United States of America

The Declaration of Independence from the King of England

Economics in One Lesson	F. A. Hayek
The Mystery of Banking	Murray Rothbard
The Creature from Jekyll Island	G. Edward Griffin
The Wealth of Nations	Adam Smith
Who's Listening	Leonard Read
The Richest Man in Babylon	George Clason
Learning to Avoid Unintended Consequences	Leonard Renier
The Underground History of American Education	John Gatto
The Pirates of Manhattan	Barry Dyke
The Fatal Conceit	F. A. Hayek
Start with Why	Simon Sinek
The Freeman	FEE.org
Secrets of Closing the Sale	Zig Ziglar
Thou Shall Prosper	Daniel Lapin